THE FUNNIEST ONE LINERS AND SHORT JOKES

JAMES CONRAD

Published by Blue Yonder Books

CONTENTS

INTRODUCTION

This book was originally meant to be a book of the best one liners, but I am afraid there was mission creep during its construction.

In the end it is a collection of one liners and short jokes. The sole criteria that was used was that they amused the author.

It was Shakespeare in Hamlet who said that 'brevity is the soul of wit'. The creation of the humorous absurdity, paradox or observation in as few a words as possible is a much admired skill.

I hope you enjoy these as much as I enjoyed collecting them.

James Conrad

Philosophy

If at first you don't succeed, failure may be your style.
Quentin Crisp

Life is all about perspective. The sinking of the Titanic was a miracle to the lobsters in the ship's kitchen.
Anon

Give a man a match, and he'll be warm for a minute, but set him on fire, and he'll be warm for the rest of his life.
Terry Pratchett

If you lend someone $30 and never see that person again, it was probably worth it.
Anon

Everyone seems normal until you get to know them.
Joe Ancis

It may be that your sole purpose in life is simply to serve as a warning to others.
Ashleigh Brilliant

Reality: What a concept.
Robin Williams

I'm not a vegetarian, but I eat animals who are.
Groucho Marx

People say nothing is impossible, but I do nothing every day.
Winnie The Pooh

Time flies like an arrow. Fruit flies like a banana.
Groucho Marx

If attacked by a mob of clowns go for the juggler.
Anon

Contentment is knowing you are right. Happiness is knowing someone else is wrong.
Bill Bailey

Look how often the unexpected happens - yet we still never expect it.
Ashleigh Brilliant

I can tell when people are being judgmental just by looking at them.
Anon

Remember, half the people you know are below average.
George Carlin

Feminism is not a fad. It's not like Angry Birds. Although it does involve a lot of angry birds. Bad example.
Bridget Christie

Hard work pays off in the future, but laziness pays off now.
Anon

Ham and eggs are a day's work for a chicken but a lifetime commitment for a pig.
Anon

Never test the depth of the water with both feet.
Warren Buffet

Experience is something you get just after you needed it most.
Steven Wright

Don't allow someone to be your priority while allowing yourself to be there option.
Mark Twain

Never pick a fight with an ugly person, they've got nothing to lose.
Robin Williams

Some people see the glass half full. Others see it half empty. I see a glass that's twice as big as it needs to be.
George Carlin

The secret of life is honesty and fair dealing. If you can fake that, you've got it made.
Groucho Marx

Silence is not only golden; it is seldom misquoted.
Bob Monkhouse

Never apologise. Never explain. – Sorry, that's my motto.
Chris Turner

We do not go in for philosophy in this country... we have our own system... it's called wondering.
Al Murray

Life is the only game in which the object of the game is to learn the rules.
Ashleigh Brilliant

LIFE

There's nothing to fear but life itself.
Richard Lewis

Some of the worst mistakes in my life were haircuts.
Jim Morrison

If you've been playing poker for half an hour and you still don't know who the patsy is, you're the patsy.
Warren Buffett

Eat a live frog first thing in the morning and nothing worse will happen to you the rest of the day.
Mark Twain

The best measure of a man's honesty isn't his income tax return; it's the zero adjust on his bathroom scale.
Arthur C. Clarke

When I was a kid, I had two friends, and they were imaginary, and they would only play with each other.
Rita Rudner

The only educational aspect of television is that it puts the repair man's kids through college.
Joan Welsh

60% of the time, it works every time.
Anchorman: The Legend Of Ron Burgundy

Few things are harder to put up with than the annoyance of a good example.
Mark Twain

Once you can accept the universe as matter expanding into nothing that is something, wearing stripes with plaid comes easy.
Albert Einstein

Blondes make the best victims; they're like virgin snow that shows up the bloody footprints.
Alfred Hitchcock

I bought some used paint... it was in the shape of a house.
Steven Wright

Ambition is the last refuge of the failure.
Oscar Wilde

She was good at playing abstract confusion in the same way that a midget is good at being short.
Clive James, Australian author& broadcaster on Marilyn Monroe

I buried a lot of my ironing in the back yard.
Phyllis Diller

I kept thinking, if his face was that wrinkled, what did his balls look like?
David Hockney, artist

I wrote a book about a transsexual with a speech impediment; it's called Man or Myth.
Stewart Francis

Right now, I'm having amnesia and deja vu at the same time — I think I've forgotten this before.
Steven Wright

Cleaning your house while your kids are still growing is like shoveling the sidewalk before it stops snowing.
Phyllis Diller

I took a speed reading course and read War and Peace in twenty minutes. It involves Russia.
Woody Allen

I must decline your invitation owing to a subsequent invitation.
Oscar Wilde

When I was a kid my family said having feelings was an act of treason.
Richard Lewis

I'm not a competitive person... I'll be the first to admit it.
Stewart Francis

If we knew what it was we were doing, it would not be called research, would it.
Albert Einstein

A human being is nothing but a story with skin around it.
Fred Allen, comedian

Sport

The first time I saw Dick Vitale, his hair was blowing in the breeze, and he was too proud to chase it.
Cliff Ellis

Ed, you're the second best umpire in the league... the other twenty-three are tied for first.
Carl Yastrzemski, American baseball player

I wouldn't say I was the best manager in the business. But I was in the top one.
Brian Clough

The batsman is Holding, the bowler's Willey.
Brian Johnston

If winning isn't everything, why do they keep score?
Anon

Driving a race car is like dancing with a chainsaw.
Cale Yarborough

Guy goes into the doctors. "Doc, I've got a cricket ball stuck up my backside." "How's that?" "Don't you start".
Tommy Cooper

I tried to start a professional hide-and-seek team, but it didn't work out. Turns out, good players are hard to find.
Anon

While playing golf today I hit two good balls. I stepped on a rake.
Henry Youngman

You could remove the brains from 90% of jockeys and they would weigh the same.
John Francome

Ice hockey is a form of disorderly conduct in which the score is kept.
Doug Larson

I never comment on referees and I'm not going to break the habit of a lifetime for that prat.
Ron Atkinson

If at first, you don't succeed . . . so much for skydiving.
Henry Youngman

The only reason I would take up jogging is so that I could hear heavy breathing again.
Erma Bombeck

I've told the players to win so that I can have the cash to buy some new ones.
Chris Turner, English football manager

A critic once characterized baseball as six minutes of action crammed into two-and-one-half hours.
Ray Fitzgerald

If there's one thing that makes me throw up, it's a dart board on a ceiling.
Anon

It's like an octopus falling out of a tree.
David Feherty, golfer & commentator on Jim Furyk's idiosyncratic swing

Isn't it fun to go out on the course and lie in the sun?
Bob Hope

The difference between being in a relationship and being in prison is that in prison they let you play softball on the weekends.
Bobby Kelton

We have only one person to blame, and that's each other.
Barry Beck, professional hockey player

Why am I using a new putter? Because the old one didn't float too well.
Craig Stadler, professional golfer

You meet a better class of person at the back of the grid.
Graham Hill, motor racer

Poland nil, England nil, though England are now looking the better value for their nil.
Barry Davies, football commentator

To me, boxing is like a ballet - except there's no music, no choreography, and the dancers hit each other.
Jack Handey

I got into the ring with Muhammad Ali once and I had him worried for a while. He thought he'd killed me.
Tommy Cooper

A computer once beat me at chess, but it was no match for me at kick boxing.
Emo Phillips

Julian Dicks is everywhere. It's like they've got eleven Dicks on the field.
Metro Radio

What's Blonde and dead in a closet? The Hide and Seek Champion from 1995.
Anon

Cricket is basically baseball on valium.
Robin Williams

I took part in the sun-tanning Olympics. I just got bronze.
Tim Vine

I was playing chess with my friend and he said 'Let's make this interesting'. So, we stopped playing chess.
Matt Kirshen

I was wondering why a frisbee appears larger the closer it gets to me. Then it hit me.
Anon

Hockey is a sport for white men. Basketball is a sport for black men. Golf is a sport for white men dressed like black pimps.
Tiger Woods

On a recent survey, 80 percent of golfers admitted cheating... the other 20 percent lied.
Bruce Lansky

POLITICS

What happens when you give a politician Viagra? He gets taller.
Anon

Democracy is the art and science of running the circus from the monkey cage.
H.L. Mencken

Politicians and diapers have one thing in common. They should both be changed regularly, and for the same reason.
Dick Nolan

Politics is the art of looking for trouble, finding it, misdiagnosing it, and then misapplying the wrong remedies.
Groucho Marx

I deserve respect for the things I did not do.
Dan Quayle

You want a friend in Washington? Get a dog.
Harry S. Truman

Mr. Speaker, I withdraw; half the cabinet are not asses.
Benjamin Disraeli, British prime minister when asked to withdraw his statement that half of the cabinet were asses

I am not denying anything I did not say.
Brian Mulroney, Canadian prime minister

Be normal, and the crowd will accept you... be deranged, and they will make you their leader.
Christopher Titus

The statesman shears the sheep; the politician skins them.
Austin O'Malley

People always say: 'You're a comedian, tell us a joke'. They don't say: 'You're an MP, tell us a lie'.
Bob Monkhouse

The President has kept all the promises he intended to keep.
Clinton aide George Stephanopoulos.

It isn't pollution that's harming the environment. It's the impurities in our air and water that are doing it.
Dan Quayle

You get the feeling that Dan Quayle's golf bag doesn't have a full set of irons?
Johnny Carson

He only had one idea and that was wrong.
Benjamin Disraeli. discussing Arthur James Balfour

Democracy is two wolves and a lamb voting on what to have for lunch.
Benjamin Franklin

The difference between golf and government is that in golf you can't improve your lie.
George Deukmejian

But there are advantages to being elected President. The day after I was elected, I had my high school grades classified Top Secret.
Ronald Reagan

There's a huge trust; I see it all the time when people come up to me and say, 'I don't want you to let me down again.'
George W. Bush

They [our enemies] never stop thinking about new ways to harm our country and our people, and neither do we.
George W. Bush

Honesty may be the best policy, but it's important to remember that apparently, by elimination, dishonesty is the second-best policy.
George Carlin

I'm all in favor of the democratic principle that one idiot is as good as one genius, but I draw the line when someone takes the next step and concludes that two idiots are better than one genius.
Leó Szilárd

You win some, you lose some, and then there is that little known third category.
Al Gore

When the Labour party announced their support for welfare cuts, they did so with all the confidence of a dog running away from its own farts.
Stewart Lee

You can fool some of the people all of the time, and all the people some of the time, which is just long enough to be president of the United States.
Spike Milligan

The CEO of IKEA was elected Prime Minister in Sweden. He should have his cabinet together by the end of the weekend.
Anon

Trump's nothing like Hitler. There's no way he could write a book.
Frankie Boyle

All those old senators going: "The confederate flag is just the symbol of states' rights." Yeah, and the swastika is just a good luck charm.
Robin Williams

Democracy means that anyone can grow up to be president, and anyone who doesn't grow up can be vice president.
Johnny Carson

His speeches left the impression of an army of pompous phrases moving over the landscape in search of an idea.
William McAdoo, Jr. about Warren Harding

We are ready for any unforeseen event that may or may not occur.
Dan Quayle

... as thin as the homeopathic soup that was made by boiling the shadow of a pigeon that had been starved to death.
Abraham Lincoln describing slavery policy

Everyone's a pacifist between wars; it's like being a vegetarian between meals.
Colman McCarthy, American journalist & pacifist

One word sums up probably the responsibility of any vice president, and that one word is 'to be prepared.'
Dan Quayle, vice president

(Extending his hand at a campaign stop) I'm Dan Quayle. Who are you?
Woman: I'm your Secret Service agent.
Dan Quayle, vice president

Why do Americans choose from just two people to run for president and 50 for Miss America?
Anon

Human Nature

The worst part of having success is trying to find someone who is happy for you.
Bette Middler

Make three correct guesses consecutively and you will establish a reputation as an expert.
Dr. Laurence J. Peter

It's better to be black than gay, because when you're black you don't have to tell your mother.
Charles Pierce

Worriers spend a lot of time shoveling smoke.
Claude McDonald

A cynic is a man who, when he smells flowers, looks around for a coffin.
H. L. Mencken

Someday I want to be rich. Some people get so rich they lose all respect for humanity. That's how rich I want to be.
Rita Rudner

Men don't care what's on TV. They only care what else is on TV.
Jerry Seinfeld

You can take all the sincerity in Hollywood, place it in the navel of a fruit fly and still have room enough for three caraway seeds and a producer's heart.
Fred Allen, comedian

I'd like to start with the chimney jokes – I've got a stack of them. The first one is on the house.
Tim Vine

While you can only be young once, you can always be immature.
Dave Barry

Confidence is what you have before you understand the problem.
Woody Allen

I have an inferiority complex but it's not a very good one.
Steven Wright

Nothing will dispel enthusiasm like a small admission fee.
Frank 'Kin' Hubbard

Those who live by the sword get shot by those who don't.
Anon

Intelligence is like an underwear. It is important that you have it, but not necessary that you show it off.
Anon

Everything happens for a reason. But sometimes the reason is that you're stupid and you make bad decisions.
Bill Murray

The only mystery in life is why the kamikaze pilots wore helmets.
Al McGuire

We are not retreating—we are advancing in another direction.
General Douglas MacArthur

The grass is always greener over the septic tank.
Erma Bombeck

Always forgive your enemies; nothing annoys them so much.
Oscar Wilde

My one regret in life is that I am not someone else.
Woody Allen

I wrote a few children's books... not on purpose.
Stephen Wright

One picture is worth 1,000 denials.
Ronald Reagan

To attract men, I wear a perfume called New Car Interior.
Rita Rudner

Every time a friend succeeds, I die a little.
Gore Vidal

Foolproof systems don't take into account the ingenuity of fools.
Gene Brown

One good thing about being wrong is the joy it brings to the others.
Anon

Patience is the art of finding something else to do.
Groucho Marx

Never trust a man who combs his hair straight from his left armpit.
Alice Roosevelt Longworth

Wisdom doesn't necessarily come with age. Sometimes age just shows up all by itself.
Tom Wilson

Never argue with an idiot they'll drag you down to their level and beat you through experience.
Katrina

The food here is terrible, and the portions are too small.
Woody Allen

Comedy is merely tragedy happening to someone else.
W. C. Fields

If a mother is laughing at the father's jokes, it means they have guests.
Anon

A conclusion is the place where you got tired of thinking.
Steven Wright

I never apologize... I'm sorry but that's the way I am.
Homer Simpson

Nostalgia is heroin for old people.
Dara O'Briain

Show me a friend in need and I'll show you a pest.
Joe E. Lewis

Common sense is a flower that doesn't grow in everyone's garden.
Anon

Few things are more irritating than when someone who is wrong is also very effective in making his point.
Mark Twain

Clairvoyant: A person, commonly a woman, who has the power of seeing that which is invisible to her patron, namely, that he is a blockhead.
Ambrose Bierce

I think hair gel was invented to make it easier to identify assholes from a distance.
Demetri Martin

Sex

Baptists never make love standing up; they're afraid someone might see them and think they're dancing.
Lewis Grizzard Jr.

Last night I asked my husband, 'What's your favorite sexual position?' and he said, 'Next door.'
Joan Rivers

Saving love doesn't bring any interest.
Mae West

My wife has cut me down to once a month; I'm lucky... I know two guys she cut off completely.
Rodney Dangerfield

I recently replaced our bed with a trampoline – my wife hit the roof when she found out.
Anon

My husband's penis is like a semi colon. I can't remember what it's for and I never use it anyway.
Mary Bourke

I sold the memoirs of my sex life to a publisher – they are going to make a board game out of it.
Woody Allen

I really must run. I'm due at my sexual addiction group, and I don't like to leave them alone for too long.
David Hyde Pierce, as Niles Crane in 'Frasier'

A mate of mine has just told me he's shagging his girlfriend and her twin. I said how can you tell them apart, he said 'her brother's got a moustache'.
Billy Connolly

I dress for women… I undress for men.
Angie Dickinson

He's like, 'Caroline, you've got a cavity,' and I'm like, 'I know – and I'd like you to fill it.'
Caroline Rhea, comedian, to her 'hot dentist'.

Do infants enjoy infancy as much as adults enjoy adultery?
George Carlin

I'm not against half-naked girls – not as often as I'd like to be.
Benny Hill

Some people are better imagined in one's bed than found there in the morning.
P.J. O'Rourke

You know that look women get when they want sex? Me neither.
Steve Martin

I lost my virginity under a bridge. I was having sex with this poor girl, and I was trying my best, but I was like Scotland at a World Cup – just happy to be there.
Russell Howard

I don't know the question, but sex is definitely the answer.
Woody Allen

I got married and we had a baby nine months and ten seconds later.
Jayne Mansfield

Oh, what a tangled web we weave when first we practice to conceive.
Don Herold

I spit on education. No man is ever going to put his hand up your dress looking for a library card.
Joan Rivers

Sex at age 90 is like trying to shoot pool with a rope.
George Burns

Boy, were we poor, if I wasn't born a boy I would of had nothing to play with.
Rodney Dangerfield

It's not true that I had nothing on. I had the radio on.
Marilyn Monroe

Broke my record last night for continual sex. 1 hour and 2 mins. Then realised the clocks had gone forward.

Anon

My wife and I went to a hotel where we got a waterbed. My wife calls it the 'Dead Sea'.

Henry Youngman

I don't think I could be gay... I just don't have it in me.

Stewart Francis

My ex-girlfriend would always ask me to text her when I got in. That's how small my penis is.

Rhys James

Women need a reason to have sex. Men just need a place

Billy Crystal

For birth control I rely on my personality.

Milt Able

The useless piece of flesh at the end of a penis is called a man.

Jo Brand

A hard man is good to find.

Mae West

Dancing: The vertical expression of a horizontal desire legalized by music.
George Bernard Shaw

I thought I was promiscuous, but it turns out I was just thorough.
Russell Brand

My best birth control now is just to leave the lights on.
Joan Rivers

Why don't you come up and see me sometime, when I got nothing on but the radio?
Mae West

The big difference between sex for money and sex for free is that sex for money usually costs a lot less.
Brendan Behan

In my next life I want to live backwards. Start out dead and finish off as an orgasm.
Woody Allen

I can't ever remember ever seeing any charity porn, though. 'Farmyard Frolics 3: A portion of this goes to a women's literacy programme in Eritrea'.
Bill Bailey

Beer with no alcohol — what a waste; that is like a nun with a D-cup.
Brett Butler

Sex and politics are a lot alike; you don't have to be good at them to enjoy them.
Barry Goldwater

You know I go to the theatre to be entertained. I don't want to see plays about rape, sodomy and drug addiction. I can get all that at home.
Peter Cook

Religion

The truths of religion are never so well understood as by those who have lost their power of reasoning.
Voltaire

My church accepts all denominations – fivers, tenners, twenties.
Dave Allen

Of the delights of this world, man cares most for sexual intercourse, yet he has left it out of his heaven.
Mark Twain

Faith is believing what you know ain't so.
Mark Twain

To you, I'm an atheist. To God, I'm the loyal opposition.
Woody Allen

Atheism is a non-prophet organization.
George Carlin

Hearing nuns' confessions is like being stoned to death with popcorn.
Charlie Sheen

Pray: To ask the laws of the universe to be annulled on behalf of a single petitioner confessedly unworthy.
Ambrose Bierce

If the Bible has taught us anything – which it hasn't – it's that girls should stick to girls' sports like hot oil wrestling...
Homer Simpson

I have as much authority as the Pope. I just don't have as many people who believe it.
George Carlin

In the first place, God made idiots. That was for practice. Then he made school boards.
Mark Twain

I asked God for a bike, but I know God doesn't work that way. So, I stole a bike and asked for forgiveness.
Emo Phillips

Why do they put the Gideon Bibles only in the bedrooms, where it's usually too late?
Christopher Morley

The church has historically been very slow to embrace technology; until very recently, their idea of a laptop was an altar boy.
Bill Maher

When you ever hear girls say that "I'm not religious, but I'm spiritual," I like to reply with "I'm not honest, but you're interesting.
Daniel Tosh

I'm Catholic in the same way, that if a cow was born in a tree, it's a bird.
Richard Jeni

It ain't supposed to make sense; it's faith; faith is something that you believe that nobody in his right mind would believe.
Archie Bunker

The lion and the calf shall lie down together but the calf won't get much sleep.
Woody Allen

Making fun of born-again Christians is like hunting dairy cows with a high-powered rifle and scope.
P.J. O'Rourke

For every little kid who still believes in Santa Claus, there is at least one adult who still believes in professional wrestling.
Doug Larson

Easter is the day we celebrate Jesus rising from the grave and coming back to Earth as a rabbit that hides colored eggs.
Adam Ferrara

An ISIS caliphate is essentially the Vatican but with less sex.
Frankie Boyle

Then God said unto John: "Come forth and receive eternal life." But John came fifth and won a toaster.
Anon

Stop taking it literally – it's only the Bible, it's not gospel.
Dara O'Briain

What's right is what's left if you do everything else wrong.
Robin Williams

Remember, if you don't sin, then Jesus died for nothing.
Ricky Gervais

Alcohol

Drink 'til she's cute but stop before the wedding.
Steven Wright

I'm not as think as you drunk I am.
Mega Jones

Ah, beer. The cause of and the solution to all of life's problems.
Homer Simpson

A bartender is just a pharmacist with a limited inventory.
Anon

You're not drunk if you can lie on the floor without holding on.
Dean Martin

Beer makes you smarter. It made bud wiser.
Franklin Jones

Everybody has to believe in something.... I believe I'll have another drink.
W.C. Fields

I don't see a beer glass as half empty. I see it as half full of hot air.
David Osmond

Those who drink to drown their sorrows should be told that sorrows know how to swim.
Ann Landers

Not one man in a beer commercial has a beer belly.
Rita Rudner

Reality is an illusion that occurs due to the lack of alcohol.
W.C. Fields

There are more old drunks than there are old doctors.
Willie Nelson

I bought some Armageddon beer, on the bottle it said Best before the End.
Anon

There are better things in life than alcohol, but alcohol makes up for not having them.
Terry Pratchett

I'd tried to straighten him out, but there's only so much you can do for a person who thinks Auschwitz is a brand of beer.
David Sedaris

In 1969 I gave up women and alcohol. It was the worst twenty minute of my life.
George Best

I was one drink away from a tattoo.
Lily Savage

BEAUTY

Don't think of yourself as an ugly person, think of yourself as a beautiful monkey.
Tanya Bianco

I used to be a plastic surgeon, which raised a few eyebrows.
Stewart Francis

I was gonna smack you in the face, but I see God already beat me to it.
Taz (WWF)

She was known as a two bagger; that's when a girl is so ugly that you put a bag over your head in case the bag over her head breaks
Rodney Dangerfield

I don't suggest that her face has been lifted, but there's a possibility that her body has been lowered.
Clive James

Where's your girlfriend? Outside grazing, I presume.
Jo Brand

Politics is just show business for ugly people.
Jay Leno

After forty a woman has to choose between losing her figure or her face; my advice is to keep your face and stay sitting down.
Barbara Cartland

Her figure described a set of parabolas that could cause cardiac arrest in a yak.
Woody Allen

She's so ugly, the tide wouldn't take her out.
Martin Kaye

I want to get a tattoo of myself on my entire body, only 2" taller.
Steven Wright

Men who have a pierced ear are better prepared for marriage – they've experienced pain and bought jewelry.
Rita Rudner

She not only kept her lovely figure, she's added so much to it.
Bob Fosse

She said she was approaching forty, and I couldn't help wondering from what direction.
Bob Hope

I'm not a very muscular man; the strongest thing about me is my password.
Rory O'Keeffe

Animals

I love defenseless animals... especially in good gravy.
Steven Wright

It was raining cats and dogs, and I fell in a poodle.
Charles 'Chic' Murray

The other day I spotted an albino dalmatian. It was the least I could do.
Anon

I'm reading a great book about an immortal dog – I'm finding it impossible to put down.
Anon

Last week my wife served me something for dinner that was so foul I gave it to the dog, and he licked his arse to get the taste out of his mouth.
Bob Monkhouse

Weaseling out of things is important to learn; it's what separates us from the animals... except the weasel.
Homer Simpson

Energizer Bunny arrested... charged with battery.
Steven Wright

I wonder what goes through [your dog's] mind when he sees us peeing in his water bowl.
Penny Moser

A snake walks into a bar. The bartender says, "How did you do that?"
Anon

The clever cat eats cheese and breathes down rat holes with baited breath.
W. C. Fields

You see I'm against hunting, in fact I'm a hunt saboteur. I go out the night before and shoot the fox.
Tommy Cooper

Outside of a dog, a book is a man's best friend. Inside of a dog, it's too dark to read.
Groucho Marx

Meow means woof in cat.
George Carlin

I phoned the swine flu hotline and all I got was crackling.
Frank Woodley

I'd be a vegetarian if bacon grew on trees.
Homer Simpson

I said to this Chinese waiter, 'Look, this chicken I got here is cold. 'He said, 'It should be, it's been dead two weeks.'
Tommy Cooper

I spilled spot remover on my dog. Now he's gone.
Steven Wright

I was watching a dog chasing its tail thinking "dogs are easily amused" and then I realized I was watching a dog chasing its tail.
Anon

As a kid I was made to walk the plank. We couldn't afford a dog.
Gary Delaney

Dogs have masters. Cats have staff.
Anon

I bought my friend an Elephant for his flat. He said 'Thanks'. I said, 'Don't mention it'.
Anon

What's orange and sounds like a parrot? A carrot.
Anon

My friend asked me to round up his 39 sheep. I said '40'.
Anon

Why did the chicken go to the séance? To get to the other side.
Anon

A dung beetle walks into a bar and asks, "Is this stool taken".
Anon

One in four frogs is a leap frog.
Chris Turner

My favorite animal is steak.
Fran Lebowitz

I said to the waiter: "There is no chicken in this chicken soup." He said: "And there's no horse in the horseradish either".
Tommy Cooper

A dog is forever in the push-up position.
Mitch Hedberg

How come when it's us, it's an abortion, and when it's a chicken, it's an omelette?
George Carlin

One morning I shot an elephant in my pajamas. How he got into my pajamas I'll never know.
Groucho Marx

So, I went to the dentist. He said "Say Aaah." I said "Why?" He said, "My dog's died".
Tim Vine

A man who carries a cat by the tail learns something he can learn in no other way.
Mark Twain

A moose is an animal with horns on the front of its head and a hunting lodge wall on the back of it.
Groucho Marx

I called the cops about a murder on my front lawn... But they said they couldn't do anything about crows and to stop calling them.
Anon

A camel is a horse designed by a committee.
Alec Issigonis, designer of the Mini car

Science

I'm reading a book about anti-gravity – I can't put it down.
Anon

I bought some powdered water, but I don't know what to add to it.
Steven Wright

In order to make an apple pie from scratch, you must first create the universe.
Carl Sagan

OK, so what's the speed of dark?
Steven Wright

The generation of random numbers is too important to be left to chance.
Robert Covey

In the school I went to, they asked a kid to prove the law of gravity and he threw the teacher out of the window.
Rodney Dangerfield

You know what, evolution is a myth; why aren't monkeys still evolving into humans?
Christine O'Donnell, U.S. Representative (Delaware)

It is impossible to travel faster than the speed of light, and certainly not desirable, as one's hat keeps blowing off.
Woody Allen

A lady with a clipboard stopped me in the street the other day. She said, 'Can you spare a few minutes for cancer research?' I said, 'Alright, but we won't get much done'.
Jimmy Carr

Schrodinger's cat walks into a bar... and doesn't.
Anon

I don't believe in astrology; I'm a Sagittarian and we're skeptical.
Arthur C. Clarke

I've seen the future and it's much like the present... only longer.
Dan Quisenberry, baseball player

Me: I'm terrified of the vertical axis. Therapist: Why?
Anon

Never trust atoms. They make up everything.
Anon

Just remember if the world didn't suck, we would all fall off.
Derryn Anderson

Consciousness: that annoying time between naps.
Anon

There is an art, it says, or, rather, a knack to flying. The knack lies in learning how to throw yourself at the ground and miss.
Douglas Adams, The Ultimate Hitchhiker's Guide to the Galaxy

I don't fall over things; I do random gravity checks.
Anon

A mathematician is a blind man in a dark room looking for a black cat which isn't there.
Charles Darwin

Logic is a system whereby one may go wrong with confidence.
Charles Kettering, inventor

If you can't explain it to a six-year-old, you don't understand it yourself.
Albert Einstein

A friend of mine was so fed up with the train delays and cancellations he threw himself on the track. Died of exposure.
Jack Dee

Everything that can be invented has been invented.
Charles H. Duell, Commissioner, U.S. Office of Patents,1899

Time is nature's way of keeping everything from happening at once.

Woody Allen

Paradox

What would a world without hypothetical situations be like?
Anon

Whenever someone says, 'I don't believe in coincidences.' I say, 'Oh my God, me neither'.
Alasdair Beckett-King

I made a wrong mistake.
'Yogi' Berra, baseball player and coach

It's so simple to be wise... just think of something stupid to say and then don't say it.
Homer Simpson

How do you tell when you're out of invisible ink?
Steven Wright

One can never know for sure what a deserted area looks like.
George Carlin

If there are no stupid questions, then what kind of questions do stupid people ask?
Scott Adams

You cannot compile a wit out of two half-wits.
Joe Orton

I promise you I will listen to what has been said here, even though I wasn't here.
George W. Bush

I hate having to explain myself. Don't ask me why.
Anon

I went to a Pretenders gig. It was a tribute act.
Tim Vine

Isn't making a smoking section in a restaurant like making a peeing section in a swimming pool?
George Carlin

A sewage farm: In what way is it a farm? Is there a farm shop?
Jack Dee

Is Knowledge knowable? If not, how do we know?
Woody Allen

Do not worry about avoiding temptation. As you grow older it will avoid you.
Joey Adams

If it's the Psychic Network why do they need a phone number?
Robin Williams

Eternity is a long time, especially towards the end.
Woody Allen

Doing nothing is very hard to do…you never know when you're finished.
Leslie Nielsen

Sponges grow in the ocean. That just kills me. I wonder how much deeper the ocean would be if that didn't happen.
Steven Wright

Did Noah include termites on the ark?
Anon

If I agreed with you, we'd both be wrong.
Anon

It's not that life is so short…. It's that you're dead so long.
Mark Whetu

My mum's so pessimistic, that if there was an Olympics for pessimism, she wouldn't fancy her chances.
Nish Kumar

Life is full of misery, loneliness, and suffering - and it's all over much too soon.
Woody Allen

If it's sent by ship then it's a cargo, if it's sent by road then it's a shipment.
Dave Allen

The first rule of Tautology Club is the first rule of Tautology Club.
Anon

Tonight's show is about doubt – or maybe it isn't. I haven't made my mind up yet.
Bill Bailey

Why can't you explain puns to kleptomaniacs? Because they keep taking things literally.
Anon

I was on the street. This guy waved to me, and he came up to me and said, i'm sorry, I thought you were someone else. And I said, I am.
Demetri Martin

I've just invented a new word: "Plagiarism".
Anon

No one turned up to the first meeting of my Sarcasm Club – despite loads of people saying how much they were looking forward to it.
Milton Jones

I bought the world's worst thesaurus yesterday. Not only is it terrible, it is terrible.
Anon

Nostalgia: How long's that been around?
Bill Bailey

Always remember that you're unique, just like everyone else.
Anon

You can't lose a homing pigeon. If your homing pigeon doesn't come back, then what you have lost is a pigeon.
Sara Pascoe

If you don't know what Morris Dancing is, imagine if eight guys from the KKK got lost, ended up at a gay pride and just tried to style it out.
Fin Taylor

The adjective for metal is metallic, but not so for iron, which is ironic.
Anon

Everybody wants to go to heaven, but nobody wants to die.
Joe Louis

How does a guy who drives a snow plough get to work in the morning... that can keep me awake for days?
Billy Connolly

Why does mineral water that 'has trickled through mountains for centuries' have a 'use by' date?
Peter Kay

I haven't owned a watch for I don't know how long.
Anon

The man who had read everything published today would be more stupid than a man who had read nothing. That's not a good state of affairs.
Stewart Lee

Being a famous print journalist is like being the best-dressed woman on radio.
Robin Williams

I've given up asking rhetorical questions. What's the point?
Alexei Sayle

HEALTH

A hospital bed is a parked taxi with the meter running.
Groucho Marx

Cigarettes are very like weasels. Perfectly harmless unless you put one in your mouth and try to set fire to it.
Boothby Graffoe.

My doctor told me to stop having intimate dinners for four, unless there were three other people.
Orson Welles

The only way to keep your health is to eat what you don't want, drink what you don't like, and do what you'd rather not.
Mark Twain

Hypochondria is the one disease I haven't got.
David Renwick

After two days in hospital, I took a turn for the nurse.
W.C. Fields

All these guys with six pack abs, and I'm the only one with a keg.
Homer Simpson

I'm addicted to placebos; I'd give them up, but it wouldn't make any difference.
Steven Wright

I used to think that the brain was the most wonderful organ in my body; then I realized who was telling me this.
Emo Phillips

I used to be addicted to swimming but I'm very proud to say I've been dry for six years.
Alfie Moore

"Doctor, there's a patient on line 1 that says he's invisible". "Well, tell him I can't see him right now."
Anon

The New England Journal of Medicine reports that 9 out of 10 doctors agree that 1 out of 10 doctors is an idiot.
Jay Leno

After the doctor finished up with my prostrate exam the nurse came in and said three words I didn't want to hear... "Who was that?"
Anon

Is it possible to mistake schizophrenia for telepathy, I hear you ask?
Jordan Brookes

I'm sort of like a post-modern vegetarian; I eat meat ironically.
Bill Bailey

About a month before my grandfather died, we covered his back with lard. After that he went downhill very quickly.
Milton Jones

I went to the doctor. I said to him "I'm frightened of lapels." He said, "You've got cholera."
Tim Vine

People with Tourette's... what makes them tick?
Jimmy Carr

Taking Viagra after open heart surgery is like a Civil War re-enactment with live ammo. Not good.
Robin Williams

Support bacteria – they're the only culture some people have.
Steven Wright

What do you give a woman who has everything? Penicillin.
Anon

A guy walks into the psychiatrist wearing only Clingfilm for shorts. The shrink says, "Well, I can clearly see you're nuts".
Tommy Cooper

Time is the best teacher, but unfortunately, it kills all of its students.
Robin Williams

My friend drowned in a bowl of muesli. A strong currant pulled him in.
Tommy Cooper

That's the thing, in a deaf class; no-one can hear you scream.
Anon

My therapist says I have a preoccupation with vengeance. We'll see about that.
Stewart Francis

My uncle was a great conductor. He was struck by lightning.
Tommy Cooper

I want to die like my grandfather did, peacefully in his sleep. Not screaming in terror like his passengers.
Bob Monkhouse

I know a guy who's addicted to brake fluid. He says he can stop anytime.
Anon

My New Year's resolution is to get in shape. I choose round.
Sarah Millican

Panic-stricken man explained to his doctor, "You have to help me, I think I'm shrinking." "Now settle down," the doctor calmly told him. "You'll just have to learn to be a little patient."
Anon

Life is like a box of chocolates. It doesn't last long if you're fat.
Joe Lycett

Went to the doctors and said have you got anything for wind. He gave me a kite.
Tommy Cooper

I'm not feeling very well – I need a doctor immediately; ring the nearest golf course.
Groucho Marx

I am a comedian with irritable bowel syndrome. It's shits and giggles.
Laura Lexx

I phoned the local gym and I asked if they could teach me how to do the splits. He said, "How flexible are you?" I said, "I can't make Mondays or Thursdays."
Anon

I've just learned about his illness. Let's hope it's nothing trivial.
Irvin S. Cobb

Patient: "I have a ringing in my ears." Doctor: "Don't answer it".
Anon

What a terrible thing to have lost one's mind... or not to have a mind at all; how true that is.
Dan Quayle, vice president

The worst time to have a heart attack is during a game of charades.
Demetri Martin

I'll tell you what makes my blood boil – crematoriums.
Tim Vine

No pleasure is worth giving up for two more years in a geriatric home in Weston super Mare.
Kingsley Amis

A man came round in hospital after a serious accident. He shouted, "Doctor, doctor, I can't feel my legs!" The doctor replied, "I know you can't, I've cut your arms off".
Tommy Cooper

A sure cure for seasickness is to sit under a tree.
Spike Milligan

A man goes into the doctors. The doctor says, 'Go over to the window and stick your tongue out.' Man says,' Why?' The doctor says, 'I don't like my neighbours'.
Tommy Cooper

Conjunctivitis.com – that's a site for sore eyes.
Tim Vine

I had amnesia once or twice.
Steven Wright

A doctor gave a man six months to live. The man couldn't pay his bill, so he gave him another six months.
Henny Youngman

I'd rather have a bottle in front of me than a frontal lobotomy.
Tom Waits

My friend was told by her doctor that she was morbidly obese... as if she doesn't have enough on her plate.
Jimmy Carr

Relatives

We had to pull the plug on my grandmother 'cause I needed the outlet for my laptop.
Dan Mintz

Familiarity breeds contempt and children.
Mark Twain

My sister's expecting a baby, and I don't know if I'm going to be an uncle or an aunt.
Chuck Nevitt, college basketball player

I didn't know my dad was a construction site thief, but when I got home all the signs were there.
Anon

My stepfather doesn't like it when I call him my 'fake Dad'. He prefers 'faux pa'.
Glenn Moore

Conscience is a mother-in-law whose visit never ends.
H.L. Mencken

I was raised as an only child – which really annoyed my sister.
Will Marsh

I'd love to slit my mother-in-law's corsets and watch her spread to death.
Phyllis Diller

My grandfather invented the cold air balloon. It never really took off.
Milton Jones

When I was younger, I felt like a man trapped in a woman's body. Then I was born.
Yianni

I am sure, wherever my Dad is, he's looking down on us. He's not dead, just very condescending.
Jack Whitehall

If I ever had twins, I would use one for parts.
Steven Wright

I'm not going to buy my kids an encyclopedia. Let them walk to school like I did.
Yogi Berra

My Father had a profound influence on me. He was a lunatic.
Spike Milligan

Friendship is like peeing on yourself: everyone can see it, but only you get the warm feeling that it brings.
Robert Bloch

"Has there been any insanity in your family?" "Yes, doctor. My husband thinks he's the boss".
Anon

WOMEN

My wife met me at the door the other night in a sexy negligee; unfortunately, she was just coming home.
Rodney Dangerfield

Rich widows are the only secondhand goods that sell at first-class prices.
Benjamin Franklin

Marriage is a romance in which the heroine dies in the first chapter.
Cecilia Egan, author

Friendship is not possible between two women, one of whom is very well dressed.
Laurie Colwin

I do dinner in three phases; serve the food, clear the table, bury the dead.
Phyllis Diller

Two old maids on a beach, streaker ran past... one had a stroke, the other one couldn't reach.
Bernard Manning

I told my girlfriend that she was drawing her eyebrows too high. She looked really surprised.
Anon

Accuracy to a newspaper is what virtue is to a lady, except that a newspaper can always print a retraction.
Adlai E. Stevenson

Paying alimony is like feeding hay to a dead horse.
Groucho Marx

My makeup team is nominated for "Best Special Effects."
Joan Rivers

I married way too young... she was Chinese.
Stewart Francis

Louie brought his new girlfriend over, and the nicest thing I can say about her is all her tattoos are spelled correctly.
Dolly Parton, as Truvy in "Steel Magnolias"

My wife and I took out life insurance policies on each other – so now it's just a waiting game.
Bill Dwyer

My wife has to be the worst cook; her specialty is indigestion.
Rodney Dangerfield

When I eventually met Mr. Right I had no idea that his first name was 'Always.'
Rita Rudner

If women dressed for men, the stores wouldn't sell much – just an occasional sun visor.
Groucho Marx

The only time a woman has a true orgasm is when she's shopping.
Joan Rivers

My friend just got a trophy wife... must not have been first place.
Steven Wright

'Mature' means old, 'athletic' means flat chested and 'not model thin' means circus fat.
Peri Gilpin

I think women who think size doesn't matter are shallow.
Stewart Francis

Love is like a fart. If you have to force it it's probably shit.
Stephen K. Amos

My wife was hinting about what she wanted for our upcoming anniversary. She said, I want something shiny that goes from 0 to 150 in about 3 seconds. I bought her some bathroom scales.
Tim Vine

My girlfriend makes me want to be a better person so I can get a better girlfriend.
Anthony Jeselnik

Will you marry me? Do you have any money? Answer the second question first.
Groucho Marx

My wife told me; "Sex is better on holiday". That wasn't a nice card to receive.
Joe Lycett

In public school my daughter was voted most likely to conceive.
Rodney Dangerfield

I feel so miserable without you, it's almost like having you here.
Stephen Bishop

It wasn't that no one asked me to the prom, it was that no one would tell me where it was.
Rita Rudner

Did you hear about the perfume that smells of nothing? I think it's total non-scents.
Anon

A man is only as faithful as his options.
Chris Rock

Instead of getting married again, I'm going to find a woman I don't like and just give her a house.
Rod Stewart

The girlfriend was molested by a troupe of mime artists last week. They performed unspeakable acts on her.
Anon

I cleaned the attic with the wife the other day. Now I can't get the cobwebs out of her hair.
Tommy Cooper

My wife just said to me "Look at this, I've had this since we got married 20 years ago & it still fits me". It was a scarf.
Anon

Curve: The loveliest distance between two points.
Mae West

She's the kind of girl who climbed the ladder of success wrong by wrong.
Mae West

She was what we used to call a suicide blond — dyed by her own hand.
Saul Bellow

I'm not saying your perfume is too strong. I'm just saying the canary was alive before you got here.
Anon

Women spend more time wondering what men are thinking than men spend thinking.
Anon

A wife lasts only for the length of the marriage, but an ex-wife is there for the rest of your life.
Woody Allen

Two blondes walk into a building...you'd think at least one of them would have seen it.
Tommy Cooper

I stopped buying women's magazines. The only time I ever see someone who looks like me is under the word 'Before'.
Sarah Millican

When we got married my wife told me I was one in a million. I found out she was right.
Rodney Dangerfield

Here's to our wives and girlfriends...may they never meet.
Groucho Marx

A man's face is his autobiography. A woman's face is her work of fiction.
Oscar Wilde

Women say they want a man who knows what a woman's worth. That's a pimp.
Rich Hall

I've got a friend whose nickname is "Shagger" ... you might think that's pretty cool; she doesn't like it.
Jimmy Carr

A woman's dress should be like a barbed-wire fence: serving its purpose without obstructing the view.

Sophia Loren

DEATH

Remember, when you are dead, you do not know you are dead. It is only painful for others. The same applies when you are stupid.
Ricky Gervais

There is no such thing as bad publicity except your own obituary.
Brendan Francis Behan

It's not that I'm afraid to die, I just don't want to be there when it happens.
Woody Allen

A thing is not necessarily true because a man dies for it.
Oscar Wilde

Saying, 'I'm sorry' is the same as saying, 'I apologize.' Except at a funeral.
Demetri Martin

I won't say ours was a tough school, but we had our own coroner. We used to write essays like: What I'm going to be if I grow up.
Lenny Bruce

Our ice cream man was found lying on the floor of his van covered with hundreds and thousands. Police say that he topped himself.
Tommy Cooper

What happens if you get scared half to death, twice?
Anon

If you really believe that death leads to eternal bliss, then why are you wearing a seatbelt?
Doug Stanhope

I hope when I inevitably choke to death on gummy bears people just say I was killed by bears and leave it at that.
Anon

R.I.P boiled water. You will be mist.
Anon

After that I worked in a pathology lab, and I was asked to leave after one of my reports said 'cause of death: autopsy'.
Milton Jones

All men are cremated equal.
Spike Milligan

Saw that show, '50 Things To Do Before You Die'. I would have thought the obvious one was "Shout For Help".
Mark Watson

Remember, being healthy is basically dying as slowly as possible.
Ricky Gervais

Will glass coffins be a success? Remains to be seen.
Anon

If he's so smart, how come he's dead?
Homer Simpson

The great thing about homeopathy is that you can't overdose on it.' Well, you could drown.
Dara O'Briain

Life is a long agonized illness only curable by death.
Spike Milligan

DOMESTIC

I've decided to sell my hoover. It is just collecting dust.
Tim Vine

I don't have a photograph, but you can have my footprints. They're upstairs in my socks.
Groucho Marx

Planning meals in advance, now that's some food forethought.
Andy Field

You can't have everything. Where would you put it?
Steven Wright

I regret rubbing ketchup in my eyes, but that's Heinz sight.
Nick Helm

Went to my allotment yesterday and someone had put six inches of soil everywhere. The same happened today. The plot thickens.
Anon

I've had a perfectly wonderful evening. But this wasn't it.
Groucho Marx

Chopsticks are one of the reasons the Chinese never invented custard.
Spike Milligan

So, I got home, and the phone was ringing. I picked it up, and said 'Who's speaking please?' And a voice said 'You are.'
Tim Vine

When people say, 'it's always the last place you look'. Of course, it is. Why would you keep looking after you've found it?
Billy Connolly

A mummy covered in chocolate and nuts has been discovered in Egypt. Archaeologists believe it may be Pharaoh Rocher.
Anon

You know you're working class when your TV is bigger than your bookcase.
Rob Beckett

I rang up BT to complain about a nuisance caller. They said, "Not you again".
Tim Vine

If anyone knows how to fix some broken hinges my door is always open.
Paul F. Taylor

I knew I was going bald when it took longer and longer to wash my face.
Harry Hill

I'm not a bath man myself; more of a cologne man.
Homer Simpson

Jokes about white sugar are rare. Jokes about brown sugar, Demerara.
Olaf Falafel

So, I rang up my local swimming baths. I said, 'Is that the local swimming baths?' He said, 'It depends where you're calling from'.
Tim Vine

My real name is Flora Margarine but I don't like to spread it around.
Bobby Ball

My friend told me he was going to a fancy dress party as an Italian island. I said to him 'Don't be Sicily'.
Tim Vine

I'm not saying my wife's a bad cook, but she uses a smoke alarm as a timer.
Bob Monkhouse

BUSINESS

A bargain is something you don't need at a price you can't resist.
Franklin P Jones

I waited an hour for my starter, so I complained: 'It's not rocket salad'.
Lou Sanders

I went to a bookstore and asked the saleswoman, 'Where's the self-help section?' She said if she told me, it would defeat the purpose.
George Carlin

If you see a bandwagon, it's too late.
James Goldsmith

Every employee rises to the level of his own incompetence.
Laurence J. Peter -The Peter Principle

Always borrow money from a pessimist as they never expect it back.
Oscar Wilde

The beginning of the holiday shopping season for men is Christmas Eve.
David Letterman

I went into a shop, and I said, 'Can someone sell me a kettle?' The bloke said 'Kenwood?' I said, 'Where is he?'
Tim Vine

Ever wonder about those people who spend $2 apiece on those little bottles of Evian water? Try spelling Evian backward.
George Carlin

I went to buy some camouflage trousers the other day, but I couldn't find any.
Tommy Cooper

Went to the paper shop - it had blown away.
Tommy Cooper

I have kleptomania. But when it gets bad, I take something for it.
Ken Dodd

I invented beach footwear for people with one leg. It was a flop.
Anon

I phoned the local builders today, I said to them "Can I have a skip outside my house?" He said, "I'm not stopping you."
Anon

Aldi shampoo; Because you're worthless.
Frankie Boyle

Bloke in Holland who invented inflatable shoes has just popped his clogs
Anon

Just because nobody complains doesn't mean all parachutes are perfect.
Benny Hill

I always arrive late at the office, but I make up for it by leaving early.
Charles Lamb

Toughest job I ever had? Selling doors, door-to-door.
Bill Bailey

Gentlemen prefer bonds.
Andrew Mellon

What if everything is an illusion and nothing exists? In that case, I definitely overpaid for my carpet.
Woody Allen

What do you call an honest Iranian businessman? Asif.
Omid Djalili

I quit my job at the helium gas factory; I refuse to be spoken to in that tone.
Stewart Francis

The difference between playing the stock market and the horses is that one of the horses must win.
Joey Adams

Invest in inflation... it's the only thing going up.
Mark Twain

We are enjoying sluggish times and not enjoying them very much.
George W. Bush

I understand small business growth... I was one.
George W. Bush

There's only one thing money won't buy, and that is poverty.
Joe E. Lewis

People are often shocked when they find out I'm not a very good electrician.
Anon

While money can't buy happiness, it certainly lets you choose your own form of misery.
Groucho Marx

I like to call in sick to work at places where I've never held a job. Then when the manager tells me I don't work there, I tell them I'd like to. But not today, as I'm sick.
Jarod Kintz

Anybody who plays the stock market not as an insider is like a man buying cows in the moonlight.
Daniel Drew, American businessman & speculator

I have a few jokes about unemployed people but it doesn't matter none of them work.
Anon

Avoid employing unlucky people – throw half of the pile of CVs in the bin without reading them.
Ricky Gervais

The quickest way to make a million? Marry it.
Zsa Zsa Gabor

I asked the IT guy, "How do you make a Motherboard?" He said, "I tell her about my job".
Anon

The man who invented Cats' Eyes got the idea when he saw the eyes of a cat in his headlights. If the cat had been going the other way, he would have invented the pencil sharpener.
Ken Dodd

The easiest way to teach children the value of money is to borrow some from them.
Anon

The closest a person ever comes to perfection is when he fills out a job application form.
Stanley Randall (Businessman)

I'm very proud of my gold pocket watch. My grandfather, on his deathbed, sold me this watch.
Woody Allen

The pollen count, now that's a difficult job. Especially if you've got hay fever.
Milton Jones

I have found a job helping a one armed typist do capital letters. It is only shift work.
Anon

I had a job drilling holes for water – it was well boring.
Leo Kearse

There is nothing more essential to getting a project off the ground than the underestimate.
Robert Brault

Not doing more than the average is what keeps the average down.
William Lyon Phelps

What the wise do in the beginning, fools do in the end.
Warren Buffett

No one's dream job involves a kiosk.
Damien Fahey

I bought some HP sauce the other day. It's costing me 6p a month for the next 2 years.
Tommy Cooper

What do you call a paper airplane that can't fly? Stationary.
Anon

Money will not make you happy, and happy will not make you money.
Groucho Marx

I took out a loan to pay for an exorcism. If I don't pay it back, I'm going to get repossessed.
Olaf Falafel

Those are my principles, and if you don't like them... well, I have others.
Groucho Marx

Travel

Milton Keynes – Satan's lay-by.
Bill Bailey

When I was in America, I really got into the culture. I went into the shop and the guy said, 'Have a nice day' and I didn't. So, I sued him.
Milton Jones

You don't eat Mexican food – you just rent it.
Alexei Sayle

I've just been on a once-in-a-lifetime holiday; I'll tell you what... never again.
Tim Vine

If opera is entertainment, then falling off a roof is transportation.
Alfred E. Neuman

Everywhere is walking distance if you've got the time.
Steven Wright

So, where's the Cannes Film Festival being held this year?
Christina Aguilera

Room service? Send up a larger room.
Groucho Marx

America is a country of inventors, and the greatest of inventors are the newspaper men.
Alexander Graham Bell

Americans have different ways of saying things. They say 'elevator', we say 'lift'... they say 'President', we say 'stupid psychopathic git.
Alexei Sayle

The global importance of the Middle East is that it keeps the Far East and the Near East from encroaching on each other.
Dan Quayle, vice president

I like Florida... everything is in the 80's... the temperatures, the ages and the IQ's.
George Carlin

The transatlantic crossing was so rough the only thing that I could keep on my stomach was the first mate.
Dorothy Parker

An Irish man who took Ryanair to court after his luggage went missing has lost his case.
Anon

Don't worry about the world coming to an end today. It is already tomorrow in Australia.
Charles Schulz

I am the only Iranian comedian in the world... and that's three more than Germany.
Omid Djalili

The first condition of understanding a foreign country is to smell it.
Rudyard Kipling

A tourist is a fellow who drives thousands of miles so he can be photographed standing in front of his car.
Emile Ganest

In Mexico, everything on the menu is the same dish. The only difference is the way it's folded.
Billy Connolly

Just got back from a pleasure trip: I took my mother-in-law to the airport.
Henny Youngman

Seasickness: at first you are so sick you are afraid you will die, and then you are so sick you are afraid you won't die.
Mark Twain

I never travel without my diary. One should always have something sensational to read in the train.
Oscar Wilde

War is God's way of teaching Americans geography.
Ambrose Bierce

What's the best thing about living in Switzerland? I don't know, but the flag is a big plus.
Anon

We had the Commonwealth Games in Glasgow this year. A great choice of venue: a place where people think Hepatitis B is a vitamin.
Frankie Boyle

What was wrong with train toilet doors that just locked, instead of this multiple choice system? If anything goes wrong, you'll be sitting there while the whole toilet wall slowly slides away, unveiling you like a prize on a quiz show.
Frankie Boyle

People who are pro-smacking children say, 'It's the only language they understand.' You could apply that to tourists.
Jack Dee

Canada's like a loft apartment over a really great party.
Robin Williams

The IQ and the life expectancy of the average American recently passed each other going in opposite directions.
George Carlin

Romanians are more Portuguese than German.
Barry Venison, footballer

If your parachute doesn't deploy, you have the rest of your life to fix it.
Anon

I'm not going to buy my kids an encyclopedia. Let them walk to school like I did.
Yogi Berra

Words

Before I speak, I have something important to say.
Groucho Marx

I would have written a shorter letter, but I did not have the time.
Blaise Pascal

I don't like country music, but I don't mean to denigrate those who do; and for the people who like country music, denigrate means 'put down.'
Bob Newhart

Euphemism is a euphemism for lying.
Bobbie Gentry

Egotism: Usually a case of mistaken nonentity.
Barbara Stanwyck

Beware of the conversationalist who adds "in other words;" he is merely starting afresh.
Christopher Morley

I wanted to marry my English teacher when she got out of jail, but apparently, you can't end a sentence with a proposition.
Anon

I'm good friends with 25 letters of the alphabet... I don't know why.
Chris Turner

Thanks for explaining the word 'many' to me. It means a lot.
Anon

Sometimes you can't hear me, because sometimes I am in parentheses.
Steven Wright

People often say "icy" is the easiest word to spell and, looking at it now, I see why.
Anon

The word aerobics comes from two Greek words: aero, – meaning "ability to," and bics, – meaning "withstand tremendous boredom."
Dave Barry

I am bravery. I am courage. I am valor. I am daring. I am holding a thesaurus.
Demetri Martin

I told a friend of mine I liked Beyoncé. She said "Whatever floats your boat", I said "No, that's buoyancy..."
Anon

I did a theatrical performance about puns. It was a play on words.
Anon

When you don't know what you're talking about, it's hard to know when you're finished.
Tommy Smothers

What thinks the unthinkable? An Itheberg.
Anon

What's another word for Thesaurus?
Steven Wright

Have you ever noticed the irony behind "hyphenated" and "non-hyphenated"?
Anon

He can compress the most words into the smallest idea of any man I know.
Abraham Lincoln

He has never been known to use a word that might send a reader to the dictionary.
William Faulkner (about Ernest Hemingway)

I was reading this book today, The History Of Glue. I couldn't put it down.
Tim Vine

Thank you for sending me a copy of your book; I'll waste no time reading it.
Moses Hadas

Ever stop to think, and forget to start again?
Winnie The Pooh

I tore some pages out of my dictionary and now it goes from bad to worse.
Anon

Ever wonder if illiterate people get the full effect of alphabet soup?
John Mendosa

Accordion to a recent survey, replacing words with the names of musical instruments in a sentence, often goes undetected.
Anon

My three favorite things are eating my family and not using commas.
Anon

Deja Moo: The feeling that you've heard this bullshit before.
Tommy Cooper

My friend Jack says he can communicate with vegetables. Jack and the beans talk.
Anon

I would never condone the burning of a Dan Brown novel, much though I loathe and detest his work. Well, I say 'work', you know, words, randomly arranged to form millions of dollars... I'm not bitter at all...
Bill Bailey

Anytime I see an autobiography on the shelf I just skip to the about the author section.
Anon

Does an earl who gets an OBE become an earlobe?
Milton Jones

Like the old adverb you can lead a gift horse to the water but ya can't look in his mouth.
Archie Bunker

'Dammit I'm mad' is 'Dammit I'm mad' spelled backwards.
Demetri Martin

Insults

She's a vacuum with nipples.
Otto Preminger about Marilyn Monroe

If brains was lard, Jethro couldn't grease a pan.
Buddy Ebsen, as Jed Clampett in the Beverley Hillbillies

When Jack Benny plays the violin, it sounds as if the strings are still in the cat.
Fred Allen, comedian

He's a real gentleman. I bet he takes the dishes out of the sink before he pees in it.
Shirley MacLaine, actress in Steel Magnolias

If you ever become a mother, can I have one of the puppies?
Charles Pierce, comedian

His lack of education is more than compensated for by his keenly developed moral bankruptcy.
Woody Allen

Am I getting smart with you? ... how would you know?
Daniel Tosh, American comedian

McEnroe was as charming as always, which means that he was as charming as a dead mouse in a loaf of bread.

Clive James, Australian broadcaster, poet & memoirist on John McEnroe

Is there no beginning to your talents?

Clive Anderson, British barrister, comedy writer, and radio & television presenter to politician Jeffrey Archer

Madonna said that "We should pull all of our troops out of Iraq". Donald Rumsfeld said, "No, I think we'd better wait and hear what Britney Spears has to say about it first".

Jay Leno

Like acting with 210 pounds of condemned veal.

Coral Browne, Australian actress discussing a acting with a leading man

Russell Brand and Jeremy Paxman (interview) was hardly Frost/Nixon was it? More like watching a monkey throw his own excrement at a fog-horn

Stewart Lee

If I wanted to kill myself, I'd climb your ego and jump to your IQ.

Shelby Mitchell, author

If his IQ slips any lower, we'll have to water him twice a day.
Molly Ivins, journalist about James M Collins US Representative R- Dallas

I tell you boy, the wheel is turning, but the hamster is dead.
Jeff Dunham, comedian

Kim Kardashian is saddled with a huge arse ... but enough about Kanye West.
Stewart Francis

The Daleks: devoid of all emotion except hate. They're like Piers Morgan on wheels.
Sean Lock

He has a body like a condom full of walnuts.
Clive James, on Arnold Schwarzenegger

Twin miracles of mascara, her eyes looked like the corpses of two small crows that had crashed into a chalk cliff.
Clive James, on Barbara Cartland

Her hair lounges on her shoulders like an anesthetized cocker spaniel.
Henry Allen, critic about Lauren Bacall

A triumph of the embalmer's art.
Gore Vidal on Reagan

For any of you who don't know, the Golden Globes are just like the Oscars, but without all that esteem. The Golden Globes are to the Oscars what Kim Kardashian is to Kate Middleton. A bit louder, a bit trashier, a bit drunker, and more easily bought.
Ricky Gervais

If brevity is the soul of wit, your penis must be a riot.
Donna Gephart, author

Don't look now, but there's one too many in this room and I think it's you.
Groucho Marx

You look into his eyes, and you get the feeling someone else is driving.
David Letterman, comedian & television host

The right honorable and learned gentleman has twice crossed the floor of this House, each time leaving behind a trail of slime.
David Lloyd George, British politician to Sir John Simon

He has all the virtues I dislike and none of the vices I admire.
Winston Churchill

If Bill Gates is worth $30 billion then a good haircut must cost $31 billion.
Dennis Miller, comedian

You look like a talent scout for a cemetery.
Henny Youngman

He has no equal. Everyone else is better.
Jason Q

She looked as if she had been poured into her clothes and had forgotten to say "when".
P. G. Wodehouse

There is less to him than meets the eye.
Tallulah Bankhead

Some cause happiness wherever they go; others, whenever they go.
Oscar Wilde

I think you'd describe those trousers as 'unforgiving.'
Graham Norton

Ian Botham is in no way inhibited by a capacity to over-intellectualise.
Frances Edmonds

His smile is like the silver fittings on a coffin.
John Philpot Curran, Irish orator

You can put lipstick on a pig...it is still a pig.
Barack Obama on Sarah Palin

That lowdown scoundrel deserves to be kicked to death by a jackass, and I'm just the one to do it.
James V Allred

An empty suit that goes to funerals and plays golf.
Ross Perot on US Vice President Dan Quayle

He is a mixture of Harry Houdini and a greased piglet, nailing Blair is like trying to pin jelly to a wall.
Boris Johnson on then PM Tony Blair

I have never killed a man, but I have read many obituaries with great pleasure.
Clarence Darrow

He is not only dull himself, he is the cause of dullness in others.
Samuel Johnson

What's on your mind if you will forgive the overstatement.
Fred Allen

He is simply a shiver looking for a spine to run up.
Paul Keating

He had delusions of adequacy.
Walter Kerr

A modest little person, with much to be modest about.
Winston Churchill about Clement Atlee

I didn't attend the funeral, but I sent a nice letter saying I approved of it.
Mark Twain

Now there's a man with an open mind - you can feel the breeze from here.
Groucho Marx

You're just wasting your breath, and that's no great loss either.
Groucho Marx

She got her looks from her father. He's a plastic surgeon.
Groucho Marx

You wouldn't be intelligent enough to understand anything that I would be stupid enough to tell you anyways.
Bill Merrill

If men's minds were like dominoes, surely his would be the double blank.
P. G. Wodehouse

Darling, when God put teeth in your mouth, he ruined a perfectly good arsehole.
Neil Gaiman

He has no enemies but is intensely disliked by his friends.
Oscar Wilde

He has not a single redeeming vice.
Benjamin Disraeli on William Gladstone

Longfellow is to poetry what the barrel-organ is to music.
Van Wyck Brooks

Lady Astor once told Churchill "If you were my husband, I'd put poison in your tea". Churchill replied, "If you were my wife, I'd drink it!"

When Edwina Currie goes to the dentist, he needs the anaesthetic.
Frank Dobson

Don't be so humble, you're not that great.
Golda Meir to Israeli Defence Minister Moshe Dayan

They never open their mouths without subtracting from the sum of human knowledge.
Thomas Brackett Reed

I told my psychiatrist that everyone hates me. He said I was being ridiculous - everyone hasn't met me yet.
Rodney Dangerfield

She's a devoted experimental jazz musician. She can do extraordinary things with her voice... not pleasant things, but extraordinary.
Graham Norton

I'm English, and as such I crave disappointment. That's why I buy Kinder Surprise. Sometimes I eat the toy out of sheer despair.
Bill Bailey

Just another nauseating butter wouldn't melt pop weasel hammered into the global consciousness like a nail of frozen piss to a cabbage.
Charlie Brooker on Justin Bieber

He resembles a cling film parcel of Frankfurter meat that's been kicked through a yellow cobweb.
Charlie Brooker on Donald Trump

She has a face that belongs to the sea and the wind, with large rocking-horse nostrils and teeth that you just know bite an apple every day.
Cecil Beaton about Katherine Hepburn

Joan always cries a lot. Her tear ducts must be close to her bladder.
Bette Davis about Joan Crawford

The Russians love Brooke Shields because her eyebrows remind them of Leonid Brezhnev.
Robin Williams

Whatever it was that this actress never had, she still hasn't got it.
Bosley Crowther about Loretta Young

She is so hairy, when she lifted up her arm, I thought it was Tina Turner in her armpit.
Joan Rivers about Madonna

Attila the Hen.
Clement Freud about Margaret Thatcher

The White House is giving George W. Bush intelligence briefings. You know, some of these jokes just write themselves.
David Letterman

Her only flair is in her nostrils.
Pauline Kael

He loves nature in spite of what it did to him.
Forrest Tucker

His ignorance is encyclopedic.
Abba Eban

If he ever had a bright idea, it would be beginner's luck.
William Lashner, author "Veritas"

Nature not content with denying him the ability to think, has endowed him with the ability to write.
A. E. Housman

She proceeds to dip her little fountain-pen filler into pots of oily venom and to squirt the mixture at all her friends.
Harold Nicholson

She's got such a narrow mind, when she walks fast her earrings bang together.
John Cantu

You take the lies out of him, and he'll shrink to the size of your hat; you take the malice out of him, and he'll disappear.
Mark Twain

If I throw a stick, will you go away?
Anon

From the moment I picked your book up until I laid it down, I was convulsed with laughter. Someday, I intend reading it.
Groucho Marx

How do you keep an idiot in suspense?

Legal

The one great principle of the English law is, to make business for itself.
Charles Dickens

I was court-martialed in my absence, and sentenced to death in my absence, so I said they could shoot me in my absence.
Brendan Francis Behan

My girlfriend hates it when I sneak up on her. According to her lawyer, she also hates it when I call her my girlfriend
Anon

I called my lawyer and said, 'Can I ask you two questions?' He said, 'What's the second question'?
Henry Youngman

Some people are alive only because it's illegal to kill them.
Edward W Howe

You can get much further with a kind word and a gun than you can with a kind word alone.
Al Capone.

I haven't committed a crime. What I did was fail to comply with the law.
David Dinkins, New York City Mayor.

Outside of the killings, Washington has one of the lowest crime rates in the country.
Mayor Marion Barry, Washington, DC.

Did you hear about the semi-colon that broke the law? He was given two consecutive sentences.
Anon

I was mugged by a man on crutches, wearing camouflage. Ha ha, I thought, you can hide but you can't run.
Milton Jones

Police arrested two kids yesterday, one was drinking battery acid, and the other was eating fireworks. They charged one and let the other one off.
Tommy Cooper

The world tongue-twister champion just got arrested. I hear they're gonna give him a really tough sentence.
Anon

To some lawyers, all facts are created equal.
Felix Frankfurter

Lawyers are like rhinoceroses: thick skinned, short-sighted, and always ready to charge.
David Mellor

If you tell the truth, you don't have to remember anything.
Mark Twain

In Scotland we have a verdict 'not proven;' that means 'not guilty, but don't do it again.'
Andrew Brodie

Let me be clear about this: I don't have a drug problem; I have a police problem.
Keith Richards

Military justice is to justice what military music is to music.
Groucho Marx

A cement mixer collided with a prison van on the Kingston Bypass. Motorists are asked to be on the lookout for 16 hardened criminals.
Peter Kay

My greatest hero is Nelson Mandela. What a man. Incarcerated for 25 years, he was released in 1990 and he hasn't reoffended. I think he's going straight, which shows you prison does work.
Ricky Gervais

In England, if you commit a crime, the police don't have a gun and you don't have a gun. If you commit a crime, the police will say "Stop, or I'll say stop again."
Robin Williams

Last Words

Surprise me.
Bob Hope, when asked where he would like to be buried

I hope that after I die, people will say of me: "That guy sure owed me a lot of money."
Jack Handy

Why yes - a bulletproof vest.
James Rodgers, murderer, on his final request before the firing squad.

I've had eighteen straight whiskies; I think that's the record . . .
Dylan Thomas

I should never have switched from Scotch to Martinis.
Humphrey Bogart

I owe much; I have nothing; the rest I leave to the poor.
François Rabelais

Either that wallpaper goes, or I do.
Oscar Wilde

I've never felt better.
Douglas Fairbanks, Sr.

I'd hate to die twice. It's so boring.
Richard Feynman

They couldn't hit an elephant at this dist. . . .
General John Sedgwick

Don't let it end like this. Tell them I said something.
Pancho Villa

The cliché is the handrail of the crippled mind.
Spike Milligan

Die? ... My dear Doctor, that's the last thing I shall do.
Lord Palmerston

Go on, get out - last words are for fools who haven't said enough.
Karl Marx

One last thing

If you have enjoyed this book, I would love you to write a review of it on Amazon. It is really useful feedback as well as untold encouragement to the author.

Any remarks are highly appreciated, so if you have any comments, or suggestions for improvements to this publication, or for other books, I would love to hear from you.

You can contact me at m.prefontaine2@gmail.com

All your input is greatly valued, and the books have already been revised and improved as a result of helpful suggestions from readers.

Thank you.

Printed in Dunstable, United Kingdom

66371921R00067